Do I Have to Go to School?

A FIRST LOOK AT STARTING SCHOOL

PAT THOMAS
ILLUSTRATED BY LESLEY HARKER

Hodder
Children's
Books

a division of Hodder Headline Limited

You are about to go
on a big adventure.

You are going to see new things, learn new things and meet new people. Best of all you will still be home in time to play before dinner.

The place you are going to is called a school.
Schools are where children go to learn new
things and make new friends.

Everyone feels a bit worried when they start school.

It's OK to wonder if you will like your teacher and
the other children and if you will be able to do all
the lessons and make new friends.

What about you?

Do you have any worries about
going to school? What are they?

It's also OK to wonder
why you have to go to
school at all.

After all, you have learned lots of new things from your family and made some friends already.

School is a place where you begin to learn about the world outside of your family...

...and the more you know about the world, the more interesting it becomes.

13

At first everything
at school may seem
strange and new.

You may not know where to find everything or who everyone is. It may seem a bit noisy and you may not feel like joining in.

But before you know it your teacher will
be helping you to learn about numbers
and counting, how to write your
name and how plants and
animals grow.

Most of the time it may not even feel like learning. That's because teachers know lots of special ways to make learning fun.

What about you?

Can you think of some other fun things you could do in school?

At school there will be paints and crayons,
trains and blocks, dolls and cars
and dressing-up boxes.

You will read stories, sing songs and dance...

...and play outside and eat your lunch with lots
of other children.

Some things may change
when you start school. You
may have to get up a bit
earlier each day to make sure
you get to school on time.

Once you are there, your parents won't be able to stay and play with you as they can at home.

But every day when you get home you will have lots to tell them about the things you did.

There may be some new rules to learn – like having to hang your coat up on a special peg...

...or sitting quietly when your teacher is talking or reading to you.

But some rules will be just like the ones at home – like saying 'please' and 'thank you', sharing your toys and not being unkind to others.

What about you?

Why do you think there are rules at school? Can you think of some other rules that might be the same at school and at home?

When you eat good food you get all you need to help your body grow stronger.

When you learn new things you give your mind
what it needs in order to grow healthy and
strong too.

And when your body and
mind are healthy and
strong…

...you will have everything you need to grow into the special person you are meant to become.

HOW TO USE THIS BOOK

Going to school is a big change for everyone, but its greatest impact is on your child. Remember small children don't have adult coping skills so make sure your child gets extra attention and care at this time. School is just one of many new situations your child will have to face throughout his or her life. Adults can help children feel more secure by helping them to know what to expect. Consider the following points to help:

If you have encouraged your child's natural curiosity and a love of learning from the beginning, school is unlikely to be an overwhelming prospect. You can help your child love learning and take an interest in the wider world simply by taking advantage of everyday opportunities. Point out colours, shapes, animals and numbers while out walking or journeying on the bus or in a car. Give your child access to magazines, books, computers and other learning tools. Regularly asking your child's opinion and including your child in family discussions will make the prospect of interacting with other adults less daunting.

The anxiety children feel about starting school is often not about school per se, but about the unknown. Some of these unknowns include changes in an established routine, meeting new children, being away from a parent for a long time, dealing with new authority figures and learning new rules. If you can, take your child to visit school before the term starts. Meet the teacher, see the classroom where they will spend most of the day and explore the playground. Anything like this will help lessen the fear of the unknown.

Even if your child doesn't express much concern about school, don't assume that means they are completely anxiety free. Not all children feel able to express their fears. Open-ended questions such as, 'Have you been thinking about what you will do at school?' can elicit useful answers and discussions. Expect mixed emotions even after your child has started school. Be sympathetic and ready to listen.

Try to associate school in your child's mind with things that are pleasurable. Emphasise all the fun things that go on in school. If your child is going to be with friends, get together with other parents and their children and talk with your children about the good things they will experience at school. In addition, talk to your child about what happened in school each day – your interest may prove contagious.

Don't forget the practical aspects of starting school. Give yourself extra time in the morning so you are not rushing or panicking. Nobody likes to start their day this way. It is also important that your child has a good breakfast each day and provisions for a nutritious lunch while at school.

BOOKS TO READ

'My First Day At Nursery'
Becky Edwards and Anthony Flintof
(Bloomsbury 2002)

'Going to School'
Anne Civardi and Stephen Cartwright
(Usborne, 2000)

'Where's my Peg?'
Jen Green and Mike Gordon
(Hodder Wayland, 2000)

'The First Day Of School'
Toby Forward and Carol Thompson
(Doubleday Children's Books 2004)

'Off to School Baby Duck!'
Amy Hest and Jill Barton
(Walker Books)

RESOURCES FOR ADULTS

The Parent Centre
c/o Department for Education and Skills
Public Enquiry Unit
Sanctuary Buildings
Great Smith Street
London SW1P 3BT
0870 000 22 88
www.parentcentre.gov.uk

Support, information and advice for all parents
and carers who want to help their child or
children to learn. Funded by the Department for
Education and Skills.

Top Marks
www.topmarks.co.uk

Website with useful information for parents on
helping your child learn and homework advice.
Has many links to other sites relating to education
and learning.